A DIFFERENT
READING

ERNEST J. HEINMULLER

ISBN-10: 1478308567
ISBN-13: 9781478308560

To: Christ Church, St. Peter's Parish – My Other Family

To: Joe & Pam

Peace & Love

Ernest Hemmueller

Dear Reader,

I would ask you to read this in the order that
prompted me to write the poems. That is, read the bible passage,
think about it and then read the poem.

PROLOGUE

In "A Different Reading" author Ernie Heinmuller invites us on a journey that some would say is a more dangerous path, since it is away from the comfort of unquestioned presumptions. One reads this book deliberately, allowing the reflections to call us to the contemplation of the awe and wonder of God who is with us. Using creative technique and intimate manner, this book invites the reader to join the dynamic of that conversation on a personal, but always shared, road; the one which is the reader's journey in Jesus Christ. We find ourselves there as the anticipated companions in an exploration of divine revelation, seeking the living God who loves. This journey is open to hearing and seeing things anew, and it does not shy away from the pain, joy, irony and wonder of life. This is a real adventure.

In reading these pages one appreciates all the more the light of God's love emanating from the holy texts. The author's prospective is brought to bear on them, and a unique witness comes forth as an encouragement to the reader. Since the truth is never exhausted, there is excitement to be known in embracing the on-going search for it. This is a constant in our lives. To read this book is to enter into a that kind of contemplation of familiar passages of the Bible for the sake of the living truth. It encourages the reader to turn the texts one way and another, and then twist them back again as one would while looking at a crystal in different light. To seek to see the whole for what it is, we hold it away, then draw it closer, and turn it over and over, to find the answers that inform the questions which inform our lives.   In this process, we break the bonds of the trap of presuppositions, and free ourselves in the faithful dialogue which is the heartbeat of Holy Scriptures. Only here will we find ourselves again.

It has been my honor and privilege to have known the author for thirteen years. In this time, I have come to have great respect and affection for him as a man of faith, grace, vitality and good humor. His company has been an inspiration in many ways. In reading his book, I am reminded that whether it is a word, or a phrase, or a moment, each, any and all of them may take on new and relevant meanings when the reader expects the text to speak truthfully, with humanity and holiness. And when it comes to being able to share this with another, it is obvious joy. This book is an occasion for truly understanding ourselves in the very best of our natures, as God intended, in real relationship with God and each other. The truth be told, it can be no other way.

Peace,
The Rev. Dr. William J. Ortt
Rector, Christ Church, St. Peter's Parish, Easton, Maryland

TABLE OF CONTENTS

Section One

Section Two

MATTHEW 6: 9:
THE LORD'S PRAYER

Our Father in heaven,
Hallowed be your Name,
    your kingdom come
    your will be done,
on earth as it is in heaven.
Give us this day our daily bread.
Forgive us our sins
    as we forgive those
    who sin against us.
Lead us not into temptation,
but deliver us from evil.
For thine is the Kingdom,
and the power, and the glory,
forever and ever. Amen

THE LORD'S PRAYER

Our Father;
Whose presence I feel.
In praise I offer you the little I have.
In this, your evolving Kingdom,
Let it be that I love my neighbor,
As you love me.
Daily I need your gift, of Peace,
To sustain me.
Heal me from misdoing,
As I seek to heal
Those who fail me.
Let me not be separated from Thee,
Bring me back when I am.

GENESIS 1: 20-23

And God said" Let the waters bring forth swarms of living creatures, and let birds fly above the earth across the dome of the sky. So God created the great sea monsters and every living creature that moves, of every kind, with which the waters swarm, and every winged bird of every kind. And God saw that it was good. God blessed them and said " be fruitful and multiply and fill the waters of the sea, let the birds multiply on the earth". And there was evening and there was morning, the fifth day.

ON LISTENING TO STRAVINSKY'S
RITE OF SPRING

In the millionth year,
Enough melted to send cold curling wave
Down curved edge of the sphere.
Slicing a small sliver from the cooling crust.
 Like popcorn, at highest heat,
A crawly thing popped out and moved, scurrying away.
 And God said,
"Did I make that –how many crawling things will there be?"
A drop, clear liquid, fell followed by millions more and quiet came.
This first gentle thing in all of such violent beginnings
A new theme moving—
an under-current to a thing about to happen.
A suspended note asking,
"God, is it finished?"

GENESIS 7: 17-20, 8: 3-12, 21-22

The flood continued forty days on the earth; and the waters increased and bore up the Ark on the face of the waters. The waters swelled so mightily on the earth that all the high mountains were covered; covering them fifteen cubits deep. And the waters swelled upon the earth for one hundred and fifty days.

But god remembered Noah and all the animals that were with him in the Ark. And God made the winds to blow over the earth and the water began to recede

At the end of forty days Noah opened the window of the Ark and sent out the raven: and it went to and fro until the waters were spent from the earth. Then he sent out a dove but the dove found no place to set its foot and it returned to the Ark. Noah waited seven more days and sent out the dove again and it came back in he evening and in its beak was an olive branch. Then he waited seven more days and sent out the dove; and it did not return to him any more.

The Lord said in his heart "I will never again curse the ground because of mankind. As long as the earth endures, seedtime and harvest, cold and heat, summer and winter shall not cease."

GRIEF

When the waters rose
    had I been there I would not have believed
that they would recede. But

they did and there was a mountain.
    A place to stand. And God
restored the seasons.

This sea wherein I now toss
    is strewn with jetsam of guilt,
remorse, self pity and more.

I, truly, need a dove, an olive leaf
    and patience to let the waters recede.
Somewhere there is a standing place. Then God,
    perchance, will restore my now darkened seasons.

ISAIAH 59: 10-12

If you remove the yoke from among you, the pointing of the finger, the speaking of evil, if you offer your food to the hungry and satisfy the needs of the afflicted, then your light shall rise in the darkness and your gloom be like the noonday. The Lord will guide you continually, and satisfy your need in parched places, and make your bones strong; and you shall be like a watered garden, like a spring of water, whose waters never fail. Your ancient ruins shall be rebuilt; you shall raise up the foundations of many generations, you shall be called the repairer of the breach, the restorer of streets to live in.

RESTORER OF STREETS TO LIVE IN

I do not, knowingly, ignore my neighbors.
I have never given much thought to them.
How many houses down the street
Does someone stop being my neighbor?
The proximity of neighborliness.
A thing to ponder.
Perhaps I should, there being in the gesture of friendliness,
The potential for Understanding to occur.
I walk down the street and notice the doors.
How much of what is behind them is locked away?
How much that surrounds me is poor?
Poor in substance, poor is Spirit.
How much is yoked in indifference.

Bring me to a fasting, Lord.
Help me be a restorer of streets to live in.

HEBREW 13: 1-3

Let mutual love continue. Do not neglect to show hospitality to strangers, by doing that some have entertained angels without knowing it. Remember those who are in prison, as though you were in prison with them, those who are being tortured, as though you yourselves are being tortured.

MENDACITY

On Sunday I come,
Sit in Peace.
Say the Lord's Prayer,
(No, I have no special needs,
it's been a good week for me.)

But,
it begins with the lessons.
"Be nice to strangers.
one of them might be an angel"!
Not likely.
"Remember those in prison,
as though you were in prison with them"

This is where you're losing me.
Isn't it enough that I pledge?—and generously.
The Prayer for Forgiveness, Eucharist.
I'm set for the week, at peace, so to speak.
Stop crowding my life!
See you next Sunday, Reverend.

LUKE 1: 26-32, 38

And in the sixth month the angel Gabriel was sent from God to unto a city of Galilee named Nazareth.

To a virgin espoused to a man whose name was Joseph, of the house of David, and the virgin's name was Mary.

And there an angel came to her and said, "Hail thou art highly favored, the Lord is with thee: blessed art thou among women".

And when she saw him ,she was troubled at his saying and thought, what manner of salutation can this be?

And the angel said unto her, fear not, Mary, for thou hast found favor with God.

And , behold thou shall conceive in thy womb, and bring forth a son, and he shall be called Jesus.

He shall be great, and shall be called the Son of the Highest, and the Lord God shall give him the throne of his father David.

And Mary said, "behold the handmaiden of the Lord; be it unto me according to thy word". And, the angel departed from her.

MARY

The Sun's
    first light was just
        beginning to wash shadows
            From my room.

I was combing,
    leaning forward,
        head bent down,
            hair covering my eyes.

When the voice spoke.
    I answered thinking
        it came from below.

But there he was
    speaking softly,
        words I could not grasp
            words I could not believe.

And then he was gone
    and my spreading fingers
        just below my waist
            knew it was all-true

In that first breath
    so long deeply held
        I quietly said,
            Joseph!

Poor, sweet, Joseph
   not to be your first born,
     not to know your trade,
      his hands not to shape wood
        seamless and strongly jointed.

Dear Joseph, how was I to tell you this?
   How would I not lose that love,
     shining in yours eyes at every glance?
   How lost now the child-dream we have dreamt.

What would you say now,
     dear Joseph?
This child I saved from bump and bruise
    is carpenter saving me. Mending broken soul
     seamless and strongly jointed.

LUKE 2: 8-14, 17

And there were in the same country shepherds abiding in the fields, keeping watch over their flocks by night. And lo, the angel of the Lord came upon them, and the glory of the lord shown round about them, and they were sore afraid. And, the angel said unto them, Fear not: for behold , I bring you good tidings of great joy, which will be to all people. For unto you this day is born in the city of David a Saviour, which is Christ the Lord. And this will be a sign to you; you will find him wrapped in swaddling clothes, lying in a manger, And suddenly there was with the angel a multitude of the heavenly host praising God and saying, Glory to God in the highest and on earth peace goodwill toward men.

And when they had seen it, they made known abroad the sayings that had been told them about this Child.

THE PROMISED BEGINNING

High in west pasture it filled the sky.
A host of voices singing of a star, baby born.
And our sheep uneasy rounding by.
How strange a thing to ask a Shepherd.
Leave the flock, and go. Now!
To break a trust, a life long vow.
For now lowly keeper of the sheep,
I, Angel of the Lord, flocks will keep.
You, as Messenger, go, speak words divine.
A Child, by Chosen Lady, born,
Will teach a rule no Age will scorn.
Then shout, Oh Israel, in your throes.
Here lies your King, born as we.
Ten tiny fingers, ten tiny toes.

MATTHEW 2: 7-12

Then Herod secretly called for the wise men and learned from them the exact time when the star had appeared. Then he sent them to Bethlehem,
saying, "Go and search diligently for the child: and when you have found him ,bring me word so that I might go and pay him homage". When they had heard the king, they set out: and there in front of them went the star that they had seen at it's rising. When they saw that the star had stopped they were overwhelmed with joy. On entering the stable, they saw the child with Mary, his mother, and they knelt down and paid him homage. Then, opening their treasures they offered him gifts of gold, frankincense, and myrrh. And having been warned in dream not to return to Herod, they left for their own country by another road.

ONE MORNING

When the baby squealed
The moment seemed fuller.
The stable brighter.
And across the space an ass brayed and shuffled its hooves.
Two cows rummaged at sparse straw.
It was all so meager, so cold.

The three, kneeling, nodded one to the other.
Now feeling the weariness,
The oft felt misgivings, of following a star, washing away.
Now knowing.
They had it all wrong!
Their trinkets, baubles and incense.
He wasn't that kind of king.
Not one the old lessons told.
Yet there was the Chosen One, there was the Child.
A story yet to be told,
Yet to be understood.
A tocsin yet to be heard
On this redeeming morning.

MARK: 7-13

He called the twelve and began to send them out two by two, and gave them authority over the unclean spirits. He ordered them to take nothing for their journey except a staff, no bread, no bag, no money, in their belts; but to wear sandals and not to put on two tunics. He said to them, "wherever you enter a house, stay there,until you leave the place. If any place will not welcome you and they refuse to hear you, as you leave the place, shake off the dust from your feet as a testimony against them. So they went out and proclaimed that all should repent. They cast out many demons, and anointed many, with oil, who were sick and cured them.

THE SENDING

Within the inseparable attachment to our past
there is a mystical moment,
when we are called to go.
To wonder what we might be.
Discovery begins every journey.
Travels with us to each by-way.
We speak with new words,
listen with deeper understanding,
find that the courage to lift the lagging heart
was always with us. And,
then, well along the way,
discover that we were the one to make the journey.

LUKE 19: 1-6, 9-10

He entered Jericho and was passing through it. A man was there named Zaccheaus; he was a chief tax collector and was rich. He was trying to see who Jesus was, but on account of the crowd he could not, because he was short in stature. So he ran ahead and climbed a syca-more to see him, because he was going to pass that way. When Jesus came to the place he looked up and said to him, "Zaccheaus, hurry and come down; for I must stay at your house today." So he hurried down and was happy to greet him.

Then Jesus said to him, "Today salvation has come to this house, be-cause he too is a son of Abraham. For the Son of Man came to seek out and save the lost."

TREE CLIMBING

This climbing a tree.
A thing that stretches
Limb, leg, skin,
Shucks off though of risk
Sees even frailest branch
A chance to go higher, see further.

How very old this childish game.
Yet.
Abraham believing
Finding Sarah waiting.
Stuttering Moses, speaking to a bush,
Gaining a rod.
Saul obeying a voice, he once persecuted.
To lose blinding scales for newness of sight.

And then, there is this one, Zaccheaus.
Called down, invited to the table,
Sharing the bread, the wine,
Seeing Jesus, seeing the task before him.

MARK 10:46-52

They came to Jericho, and as he and his disciples and a large crowd were leaving Jericho, Bartimaeus son of Timaeus, a blind beggar, was sitting by the roadside. When he heard it was Jesus of Nazareth he began to shout out and say, "Jesus, Son of David, have mercy on me!" Many sternly ordered him to be quiet, but he cried out even more loudly, "Son of David, have mercy on me!" Jesus stood still and said, "Call him here." And they called the blind man, saying to him, take heart, get up, he is calling you." So throwing of his cloak he sprang up and came to Jesus. Then Jesus said to him, "What do you want me to do for you?" The blind man said, "My teacher, let me see again." Jesus said to him, "Go: your faith has made you well." Immediately he regained his sight and followed him on his way.

AND JESUS STOOD STILL

In this hustle-bustle of Life
Jostled by cares, grief, unreasoned want,
Avarice and, yes, people that crowd
Into our ever moving lives why
Can't we stand still?

There was that persistent Grace of God
Raising a blind one's voice.
And, it was heard by the One,
Who stopped,
Did a good thing and went on.

Perhaps therin is our answer.
That persistent Grace,
Raising voices all around,
Waiting for us to stand still and listen.

LUKE 22:54-62

Then they seized him and led him away, bringing him into the high priest's house. But Peter was following at a distance. When they had kindled a fire in the middle of the courtyard and sat together, Peter sat among them. Then a servant-girl seeing him in the firelight stared at him and said, "This man also was with him." But he denied it, saying, "Woman, I do not know him." A little later someone else on seeing him said, "You also are one of them." But Peter said, "Man, I am not." Then about an hour later still another kept insisting, "Surely, this man was with him, for he is a Galilean." But Peter said, "Man, I do not know what you are talking about." At that moment while he was still speaking, the cock crowed. The Lord turned and looked at Peter. Then Peter remembered how the Lord had said to him, "Before the cock crows today, you will deny me three times." And he went away and wept bitterly.

SEPARATION

Consider this for a moment.
In their dark, dark world
a blind person's sense of space
is zero. No nearness, farness,
Up, down, across, here nor there. One
lives a life separated. And,

So it was with them.
Judas
Peter
All the others.
Moving even farther away from the missing One,
in that physical, spiritual darkness that
came over them.
Leaving each apart, one from the other,
with nothing to be trusted.
Nothing, that is, but a promise.
Something will happen in three days.
Will it be enough?

Are there such tests of faith?
Watch there.
A tapping of white stick to curb.

ACTS 7: 54-60

When they heard these things, they became enraged and ground their teeth at Stephen.

But filled with the Holy Spirit he gazed into Heaven and saw the glory of God and Jesus standing at the right hand of God. "Look," he said, "I see the Heavens opened and the Son of Man standing at the right hand of God." But they covered their ears, and with a loud shout all rushed together against him. Then they dragged him out of the city and began to stone him: and the witnesses laid their coats at the feet of Saul. While they were stoning Stephen he prayed, "Lord Jesus, receive my spirit." Then he knelt down and cried out in a loud voice, "Lord, do not hold this sin against them." When he had said this he died. And Saul approved of their killing him.

STEPHEN

When the stone was cast,
Without thought of action,
Strange, it struck a man.

MARK 15: 21-22

As they led him away, they came upon a man of Cyrene , Simon by name, who was coming from the country, and laid on him the cross to carry it behind Jesus "If anyone would come after me, let him deny himself and take up his cross and follow me. Take my yoke upon you, and learn from me, for my yoke is easy, and my burden is light."

SERENDIPITY

Blushing sky chases Night westward
Signaling day.
How simple this beginning.
Marked by world's turning,
In measured time.
Washing away Yesterday's print,
Laying clean path for new journeys.
What lies there?

Shake loose sleep.
Wash at ancient well's spill-trough.
Do prayers from unnumbered days.
Hurry along, I have need of thee,
Simon of Cyrene.

Ah, Simon, just as I stumble
There you are!

Something there is here,
More than cross-lashed wood
I give you to carry.
Bear it to the Hill and—
And beyond.
Never again will you be yesterday's
Simon of Cyrene.

JOHN 19:17-19

So they took Jesus and carrying the cross by himself, he went out to what is called the place of the Skulls, which in Hebrew is called Golgotha. There they crucified him, and with him two others, one on each side.

THE CROSS

Striking nails
  send sharp sound
through fine grain of cross beam. One

ask of this awful use,
  was it for this
against Lebanon's westerly winds

it grew branch and leaf? Never bending,
  rooted tendrils deep
to grow stronger each year.

This ironic use of Father's creation.

Strange, use for all things lies but finger touch away.
  For larger need one thing grew---
    one thing died.

What is this about Purpose
  that wrong is so oft made of it?
And yet, this using leads me
  beyond understanding to Acceptance.

MATTHEW 17: 39-44

And they that passed by reviled him, wagging their heads, and saying, Thou that would destroy the Temple, and build it in three days, save yourself. If thou be the Son of God, come down from the cross.
Likewise the chief priest mocking him with the scribes and elders; said; He saved others himself he cannot save. If he be the King of Israel, let him now come down from the cross, and we will believe him. The thieves also cast the same in his teeth.

SOMETHING TO DO ON FRIDAY

There were indeed, three crosses.
Yes three, two facing the middle one.
One, a fellow perhaps worthy of pity.
So pathetic his fright,
Well, actually weeping, completely to pieces.
Yet talking to the one in the middle.
On the other hand there was the one to the left
Dying and yet spending breath in curses and laughter.
He was for awhile, the crowd's favorite.
The one in the middle…

A quiet man.
Not one you'd watch.
Not one you'd watch at all, really.
No, I mean, certainly after the long walk to the hill,
No, not one you'd watch being crucified.

JOHN 19: 23-24

Then the soldiers when they had crucified Jesus
took his garments and made four parts, to every
soldier a part; and also his coat; now the coat
was without seam, woven from the top without seam.

They said therefore among themselves, "Let us
not rend it, but cast lots for it". So the scripture was fulfilled that saith,
they parted my raiment and cast lots for my coat.

CASTING LOTS AT GOLGOTHA

A man is going to die here.
And in a thousand years,
Maybe two thousand years
The grass will be green again.
People will say, "It wasn't
What you thought it was."
But it was.
That thing of living by the Law.
A narrow-spirited existence
Harboring Humanity and Inhumanity
Both in the name of Justice.
And, there we were rejecting Grace.
Even, when it was only a last cry away.
So, there is this.
The grass is green now.
And,
The warriors are nameless.

MATTHEW 26: 26-28

And as they were eating Jesus took bread and blessed it, and brake it, and gave it to the disciples, and said, "Take, eat ; this is my body." And he took the cup, and gave thanks, and gave it to them, saying, "Drink ye all of it." For this is my blood of the new testament which is shed for the many for the remission of sins."

EUCHARIST

Ushers invite us.
There are forty-six steps from my seat
    To the table

A space of countless Time.
Defined, holding questions, apprehensions,
    And then, I am kneeling

Two servers, dear friends.
"Ernie, this is my body."
"Ernie, this my blood."
Whose voice did I hear?

Now my steps retraced.
Kneeling, I muse.
Perhaps, yes perhaps,
It was a foolish question.

SECTION II

THE STATIONS OF THE CROSS

It seems fitting, here, to use haiku poetry as the response form - as the Stations of the Cross are condensed, so is the form Haiku. A poem in three lines using seventeen syllables.

THE FIRST STATION

As soon as it was morning, the chief priest, with the elders and scribes, and the whole council, held a consultation; and they bound Jesus and led him away and delivered him to Pilate. And they all condemned him and said, "He deserves to die."

JESUS IS CONDEMNED TO DIE

And the ones Condemning
Unjustly without reason.
Know who is being condemned.

THE SECOND STATION

Jesus went out, bearing his own cross on the way to the place called the place of a skull, in Hebrew, Golgotha. Although he was a Son, he learned obedience through what he suffered. Like a lamb he was led to the slaughter; and like a sheep that before its shearers is mute, so he opened not his mouth. Worthy is the Lamb who was slain, to receive power and riches and wisdom and strength and honor and glory and blessing.

JESUS TAKES UP HIS CROSS

This mute acceptance.
Shearing, a purpose of birth.
Clothes me in Love.

THE THIRD STATION

Christ Jesus, though he was in the form of God, did not count equality with God a thing to be grasped; but emptied himself, taking the form of a servant, and was born in human likeness. And being found in human form he humbled himself and became obedient unto death, even death on a cross. Therefore God has highly exalted him, and bestowed on him the name which is above every name. Come let us bow down, and bend the knee, and kneel before the Lord our Maker, for he is the Lord our God.

JESUS FALLS THE FIRST TIME

If I would seek Christ
There is first the hard thing.
I must learn to kneel.

THE FOURTH STATION

We adore you, 0 Christ, and we bless you:
Because by your holy cross you have redeemed the world.

To what can I liken you, to what can I compare you, 0 daughter of Jerusalem? What likeness can I use to comfort you, 0 virgin daughter of Zion? For vast as the sea is your ruin. Blessed are those who mourn, for they shall be comforted. The Lord will be your everlasting light, and your days of mourning shall be ended.

JESUS MEETS HIS AFFLICTED MOTHER

Things appearing in ruin
Rise on the strength of promise.
Quiet the solitary cry.

THE FIFTH STATION

As the led him away, they came upon a man of Cyrene , Simon by name, who was coming from the country, and laid on him the cross to carry it behind Jesus "If anyone would come after me, let him deny himself and take up his cross and follow me. Take my yoke upon you, and learn from me, for my yoke is easy, and my burden is light."

THE CROSS IS LAID ON SIMON

Lifting the burden
Muscles flex, bend to the task.
My Spirit rising.

THE SIXTH STATION

We have seen him without beauty or majesty, with no looks to attract the eye. He was despised and rejected by men ; a man of sorrows, and acquainted with grief; and as one from whom men hide their faces, he was despised, and we esteemed him not. His appearance was so marred, beyond human semblance, and his form beyond that of the children of men. But he was wounded for our transgressions, he was bruised for our iniquities, upon him was the chastisement that made us whole, and with his stripes we are healed.

A WOMAN WIPES HIS FACE

Reaching for his face
His eyes told me there was more
But, grief blinded me.

THE SEVENTH STATION

Surely he has borne our grief and carried our sorrows. All we like sheep have gone astray; we have turned every one to his way; and the Lord has laid on him the iniquity of us all. He was opposed, and he was afflicted, yet he opened not his mouth. For the transgressions of my people he was stricken.

JESUS FALLS THE SECOND TIME

The strength of Silence
in the midst of duty's call
Speaks to acceptance.

THE EIGHTH STATION

There followed after Jesus a great multitude of the people, and among them were grief stricken women who followed close by Jesus on his journey to Calvary. But Jesus turned their focus away from Himself and said, "Daughters of Jerusalem, do not weep for me, but weep for yourselves and for your children."

JESUS MEETS THE WOMEN OF JERUSALEM

Mourning, a sound soft
As willow's wind moved sigh.
A calling for Hope.

THE NINTH STATION

I am the man who has seen affliction under the rod of his wrath; he has driven and brought me into darkness without any light. He has besieged me and enveloped me with bitterness and tribulation; he has made me dwell in darkness like the dead of long ago. Though I call and cry for help, he shuts out my prayer. He has made my teeth grind on gravel, and made me cower in ashes."Remember, O Lord, my affliction and bitterness, the wormwood and the gall!"

REMEMBER O LORD MY AFFLICTION

In that darkest time
Is it Thee, not listening,
Or me, not hearing?

THE TENTH STATION

When they came to a place called Golgotha (which means the place of the skull), they offered him wine to drink, mingled with gall; but when he tasted it, he would not drink it. And they divided his garments among them by casting lots. This was to fulfill the scripture which says, "They divided my garments among them; they cast lots for my clothing."

JESUS IS STRIPPED OF HIS GARMENTS

Autumn leaves falling
Expose tree to cruel Winter.
But wait, Spring triumphs.

THE ELEVENTH STATION

When they came to the place which is called The Skull, there they crucified him; and with him they crucified two criminals, one on the right, the other on the left, and Jesus between them. And the scripture was fulfilled which says, "He was numbered with the transgressors."

JESUS IS NAILED TO THE CROSS

Look here! See my wrist.
Marked by the true transgressors.
There for every Thomas.

THE TWELFTH STATION

When Jesus saw his mother, and the disciple whom he loved standing near, he said to his mother, "Woman, behold your son!" Then he said to the disciple, "Behold your mother!" And when Jesus received the vinegar, he said, "It is finished!" And then crying with a loud voice, he said "Father, into your hands I commend my spirit." and he bowed his head, and handed over his spirit.

JESUS DIES ON THE CROSS

My God, my God, why?
A cry blowing in the wind
Echoing, echoing still.

THE THIRTEENTH STATION

All you who pass by, behold and see if there is any sorrow like my sorrow. My eyes are spent with weeping; my soul is in tumult; my heart is poured out in grief because of the downfall of my people."Do not call me Naomi (which means Pleasant), call me Mara (which means Bitter); for the Almighty has dealt very bitterly with me.

MARY'S LAMENT

Where is my Angel, Lord?
I said, "Here I am." You blest me.
Bitterness fills my heart.

THE FOURTEENTH STATION

When it was evening, there came a rich man from
Arimathea, named Joseph, who also was a disciple of Jesus. He went
to Pilate and asked for the body of Jesus. Then Pilate ordered it given
to him. And, Joseph took the body and wrapped it in a clean linen
shroud, and laid it in his own new tomb, which he had hewn in the
rock; and he rolled a great stone to the door of the tomb.

AT THE TOMB

Symbol of finality
There's a promise to be kept.
Moving more than stone.

ACKNOWLEDGEMENTS

This book was begun with an appreciation that poems have been written throughout the ages of literature that are truly a broad voice for the Bible Message. I will always be grateful to these people I now sincerely thank. Reverend Carol Callaghan has been mentor and teacher through each piece written. The Lent and Advent readings assembled by Rev. Callaghan and Kitty Bayh have further enhanced my thinking that poetry is a voice from which willing listeners can learn. The reading-team of Kitty Bayh and Dick Welch are gratefully acknowledged. The expert work of Joanne Fisher (Youth & Family Minister) in assembling and formatting each page has been more than appreciated. I consider that the prologue written by the Rev. Dr. William Ortt, Rector of Christ Church, Easton, Maryland, a gift to me that more than ever binds me to serve his church and work. The cover is a painting I did some years ago at the beach.

Made in the USA
Charleston, SC
27 September 2012